MEL BAY PRESENTS

IRISH MUSIC FOR MANDOLIN
MADE EASY
BY PHILIP JOHN BERTHOUD

CD Contents

1. Factory Girl (Air)
2. Paddy's Green Shamrock Shore (Air)
3. Planxty Irwin (Air)
4. Carolan's Dream (Air)
5. The Parting of Friends (Air)
6. The Derry Air (Air)
7. The Star of the County Down (Air)
8. Whiskey in the Jar (Air)
9. Oh! The Britches Full of Stitches (Polka)
10. John Ryan's (Polka)
11. Kerry Polka (Polka)
12. The Rakes of Mallow (Polka)
13. The Road to Lisdoonvarna (Slide)
14. Tatter the Road (Slide)
15. The Runaway Jig (Slide)
16. The Butterfly (Slip Jig)
17. The Rocky Road to Dublin (Slip Jig)
18. The Rakes of Westmeath (Slip Jig)
19. The Irish Washerwoman (Jig)
20. Caliope House (Jig)
21. The Cliffs of Moher (Jig)
22. Sergeant Early's Jig (Jig)
23. The Jolly Beggarman (Hornpipe)
24. The Rights of Man (Hornpipe)
25. The Wren Hornpipe (Hornpipe)
26. The Boys of Malin (Reel)
27. Miss McLeod's Reel (Reel)
28. The Merry Blacksmith (Reel)
29. The Star of Munster (Reel)

GW00580123

1 2 3 4 5 6 7 8 9 0

Visit us on the Web at www.melbay.com — E-mail us at email@melbay.com

Table of Contents

Introduction

This book and recording contains a selection of 29 traditional Irish tunes. They are arranged for easy mandolin, roughly in order of difficulty. The music is clear and easy to read, but for those that don't read music, the music is written in mandolin tablature as well as standard notation. Some readers may be unfamiliar with **first time endings** and **second time endings**. Look at Paddy's Green Shamrock Shore on page 5 and notice the brackets containing the figures 1 and 2 halfway along the third line of music. Imagine you are playing the tune and you come to the first bracket with the number 1 in it – this is the first time ending. Play the two bars under this bracket and you'll reach the repeat barline (double line with two dots), which tells you to repeat this section (from the third bar of line 2). Now you're playing this music for the second time, which means that you'll *skip* the first time ending when you come to it and jump straight to the second time ending (the bracket with the 2 in it). First time endings are also known as first time bar or first time bars – likewise for second time endings. None of the tunes rise higher than the seventh fret. Each tune is featured on the accompanying recording, played through at a slow tempo 2 or 3 times.

When working on a particular tune, spend time listening to the recording, in order to familiarize yourself with the sound of the tune. With traditional music, a great deal is picked up by ear. Have the tune going round in your head before attempting to play it. This will make the process more natural and rewarding.

On the recording, each new tune will be "tapped-in" so that you know when the music will start. Aim to play along with the recording as soon as you know a tune well. They are all recorded quite slowly so as to make playing along more manageable.

With traditional Irish music it is quite normal to play a particular tune through more than once. In some of the tunes in this book you will find a final note/notes printed in brackets – these notes are designed to be left out when playing a tune for the last time. They are only played if you are going to go back to the beginning of a tune and repeat it. Likewise, some tunes are shown with a single note at the end that is clearly marked to be played the last time through.

Below is an effective plan of action for tackling each new tune:

1. Listen to the tune on the recording a couple of times.

2. Listen to the tune again, this time following the corresponding music in the book.

3. Look more carefully at the music and make sure you understand what you need to do to play it.

4. Now, working at your own pace, begin to play the tune. How slow or fast you go is not important. What is important is that you take care to play the right notes.

5. Check the recording to hear what it should sound like.

6. Keep practicing the tune, getting to know it better.

7. When you are at the stage that you can play the tune from beginning to end, you could try playing along with the recording. If you don't get to the end, don't worry. Set yourself targets such as reaching the end of the first line, then the second line of music.

8. When you know it well, see how much you can play by memory. Some players do this more naturally than others.

Thanks to Dave Wade for mixing and mastering the recording.

Factory Girl

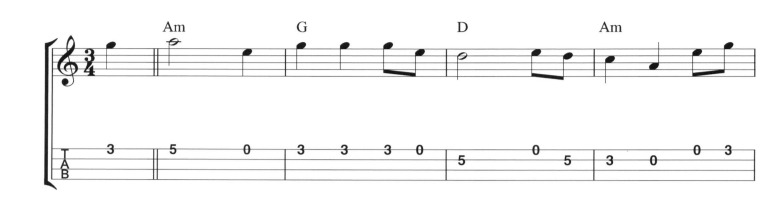

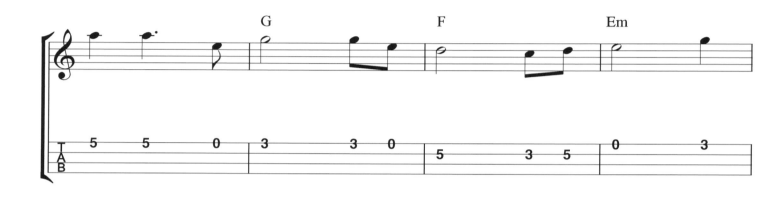

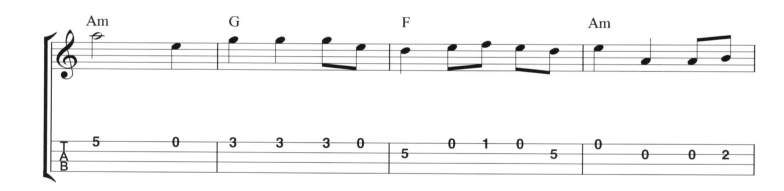

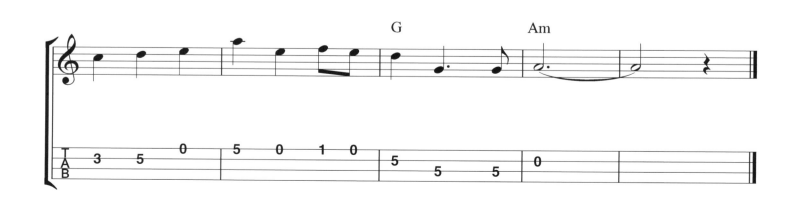

Paddy's Green Shamrock Shore

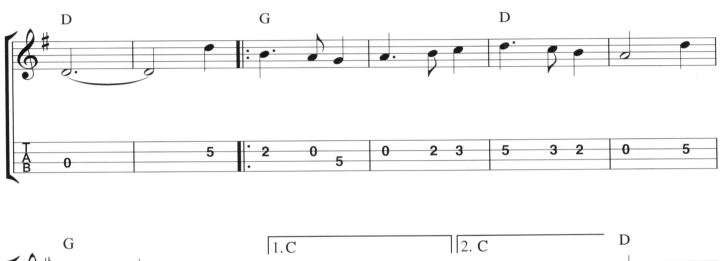

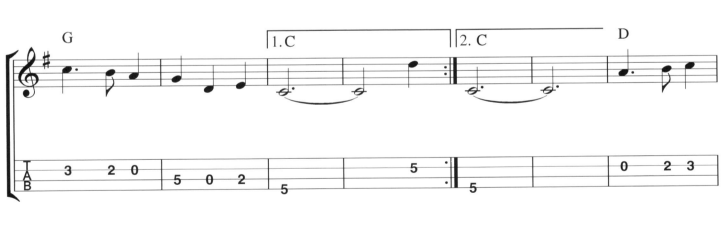

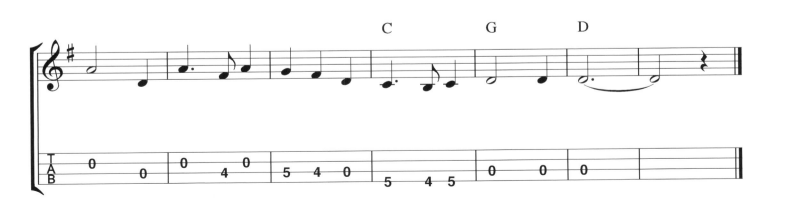

Planxty Irwin

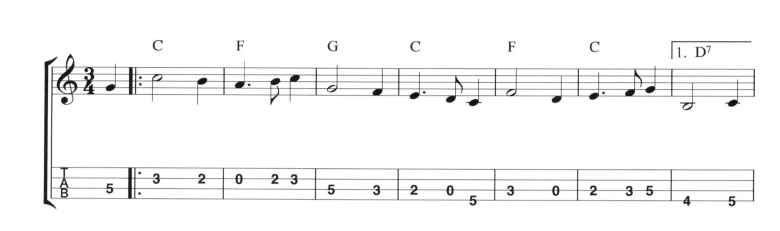

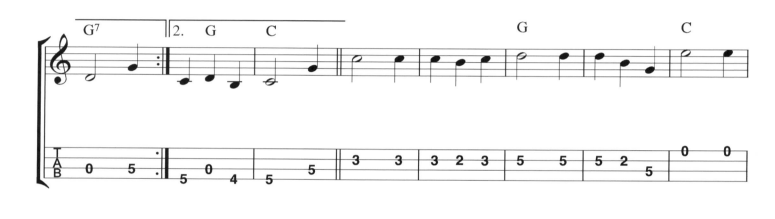

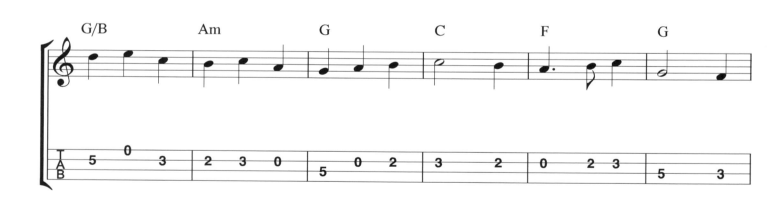

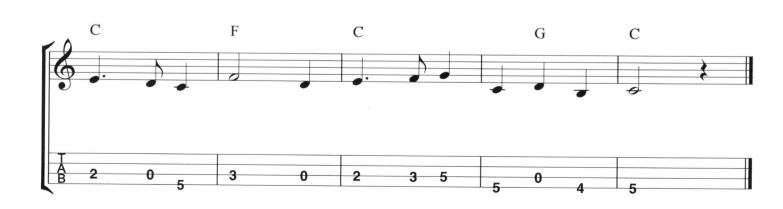

Carolan's Dream

The Parting of Friends

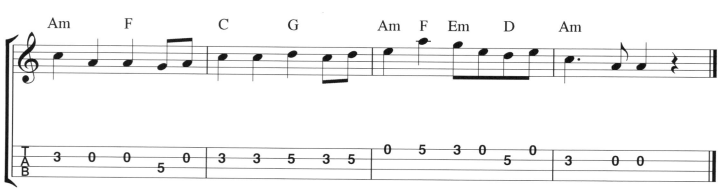

The Derry Air

The Star of the County Down

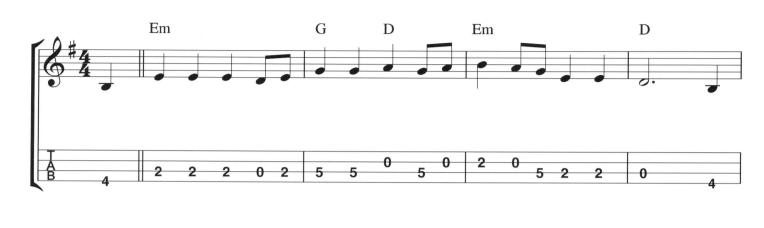

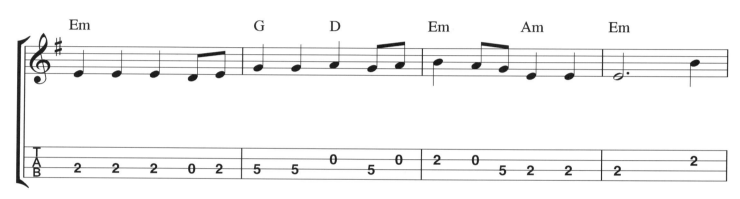

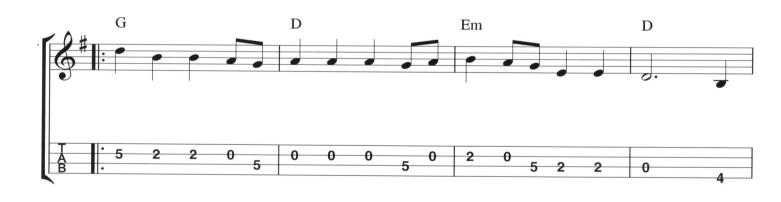

Whiskey in the Jar

The Britches Full of Stitches

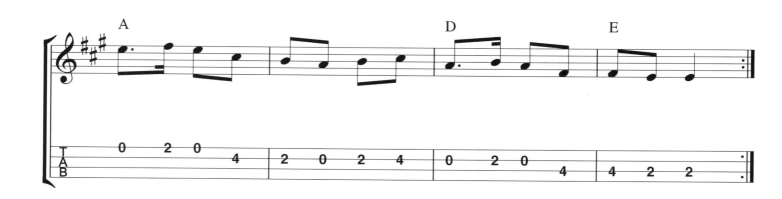

John Ryan's Polka

Kerry Polka

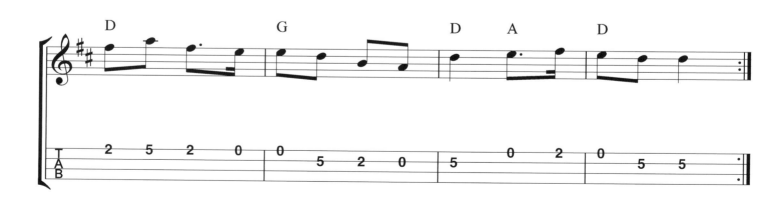

The Rakes of Mallow

The Road to Lisdoonvarna

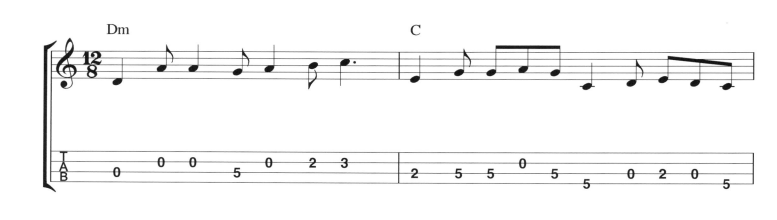

Tatter the Road

The Runaway Jig

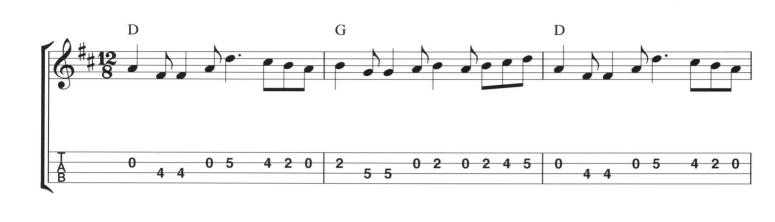

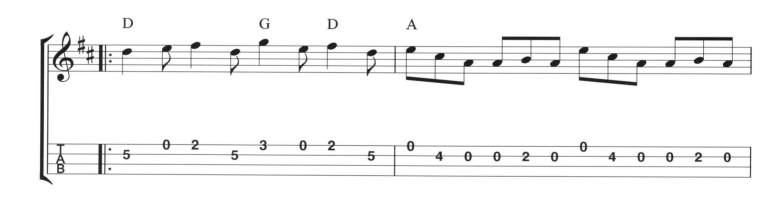

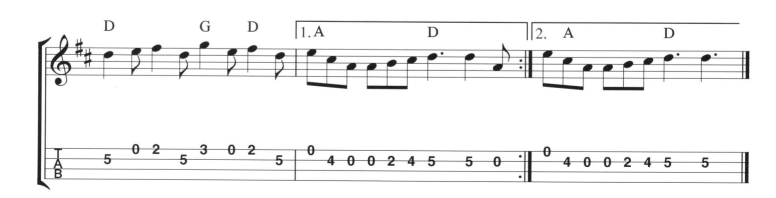

The Butterfly

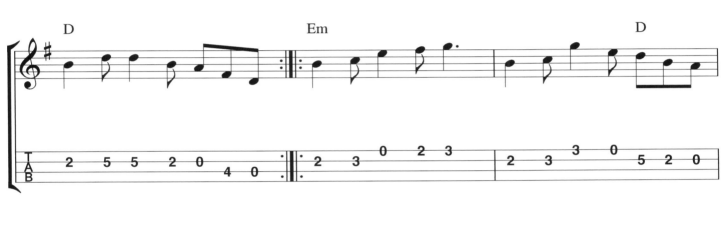

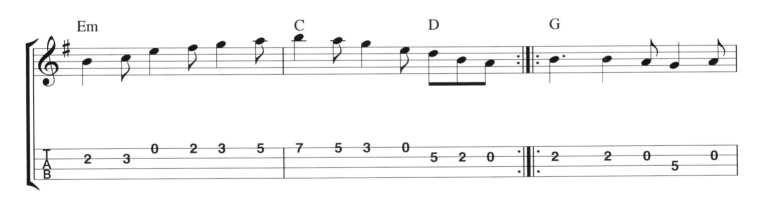

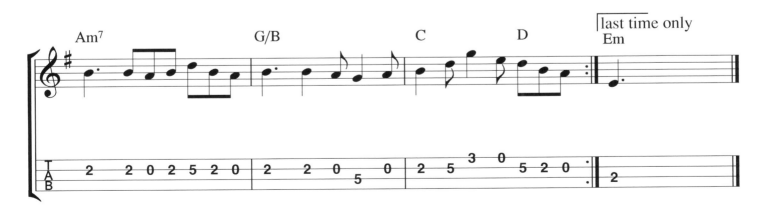

The Rocky Road to Dublin

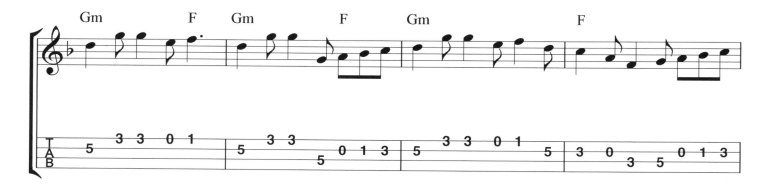

The Rakes of Westmeath

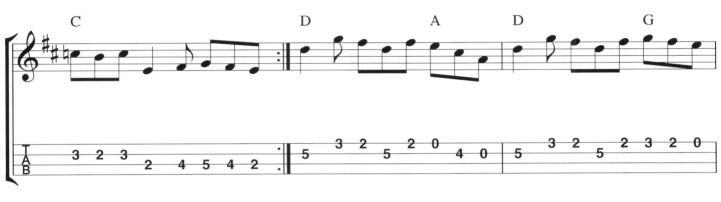

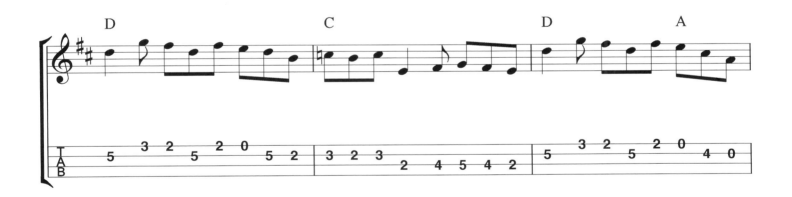

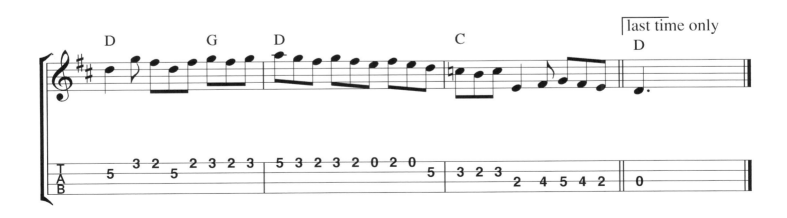

The Irish Washerwoman

Caliope House

The Cliffs of Moher

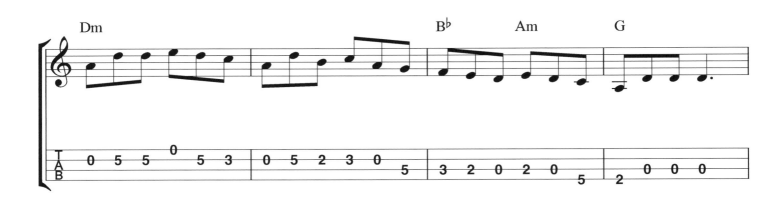

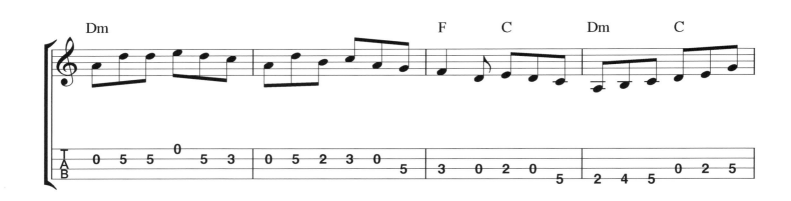

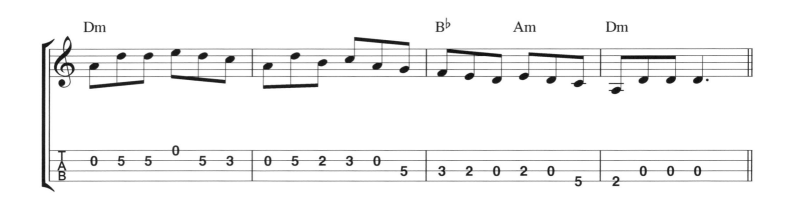

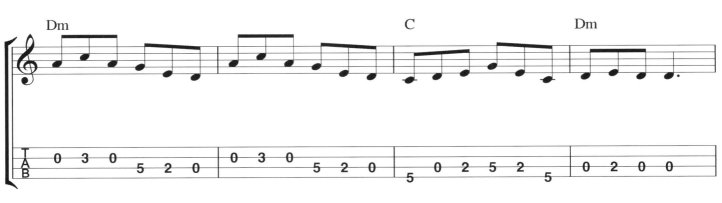

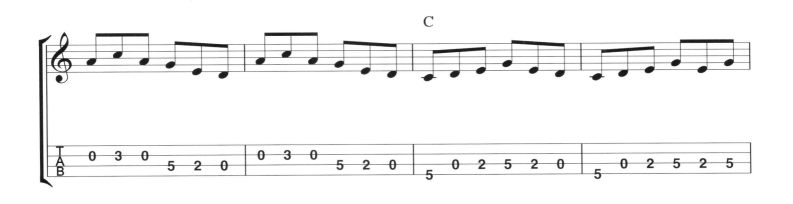

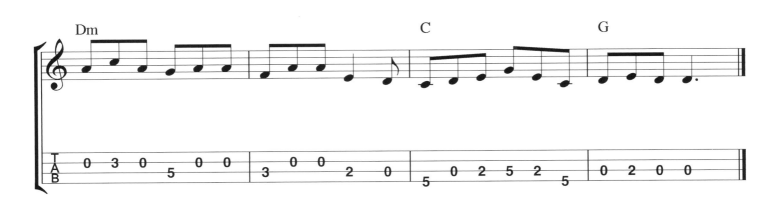

This page has been left blank
to avoid awkward page turns.

Sergeant Early's Jig

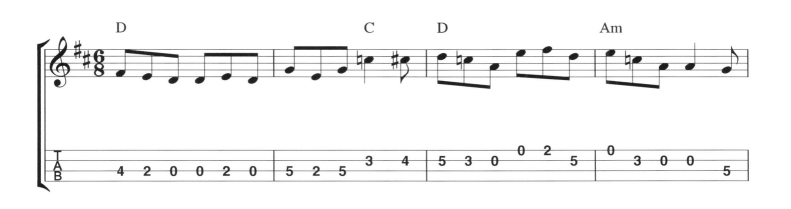

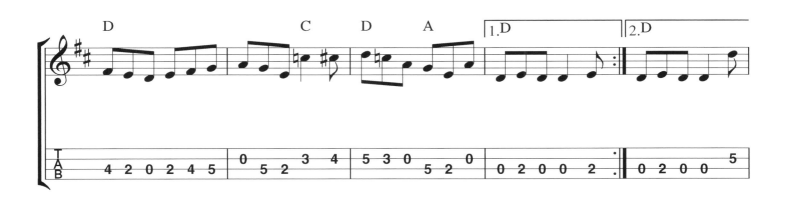

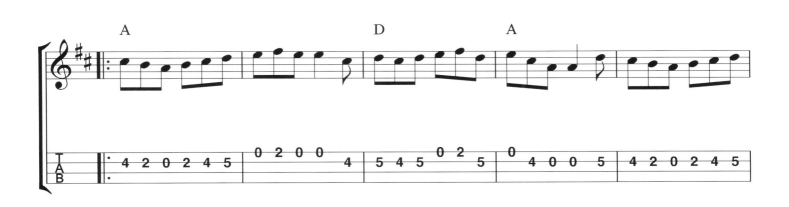

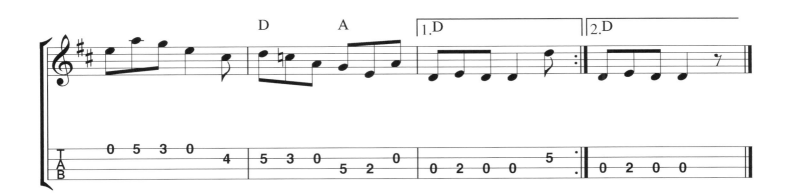

The Jolly Beggarman

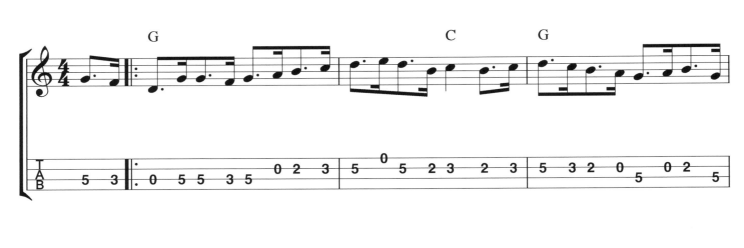

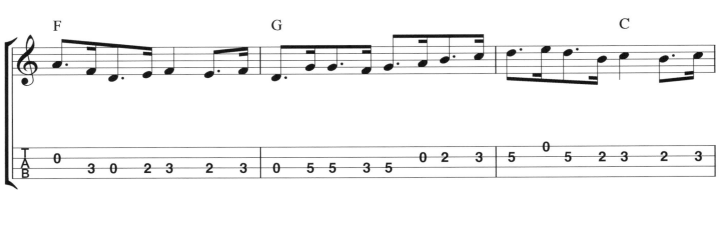

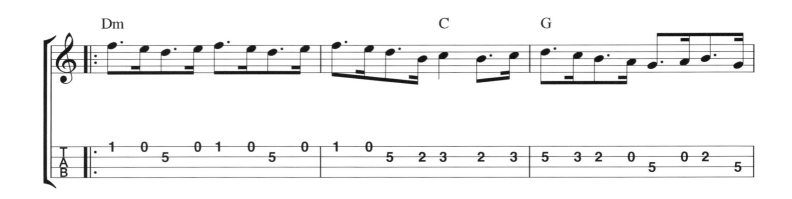

The Rights of Man

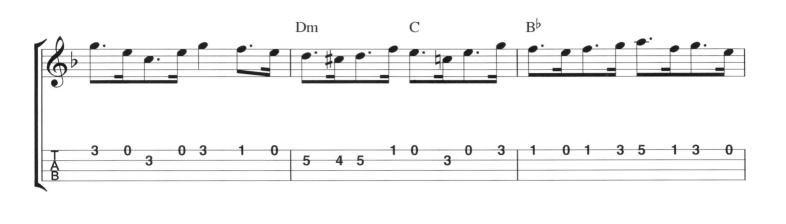

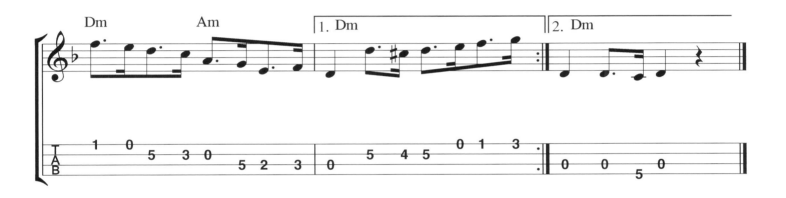

The Wren Hornpipe

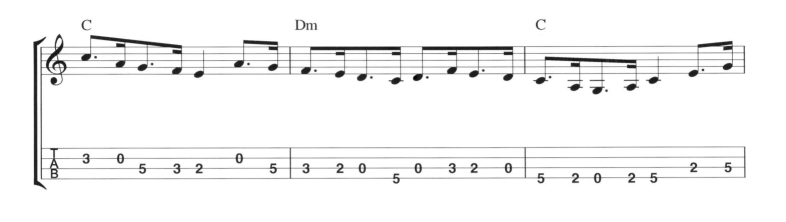

The Boys of Malin

Miss McLeod's Reel

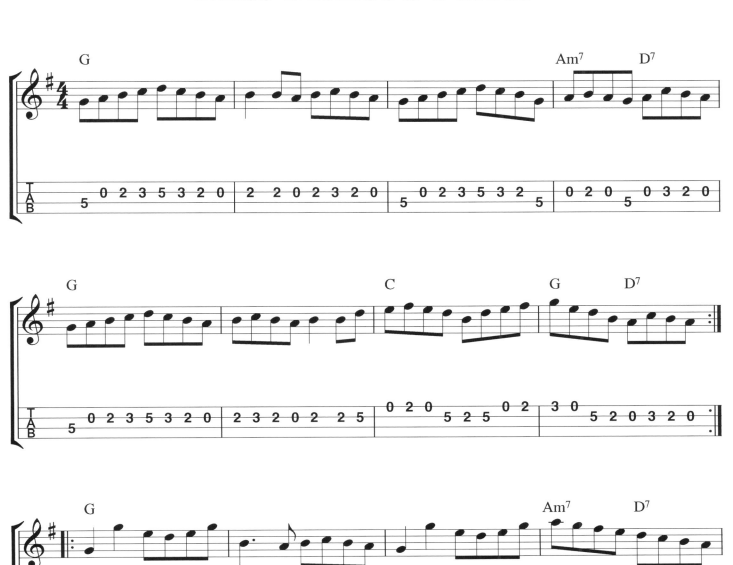

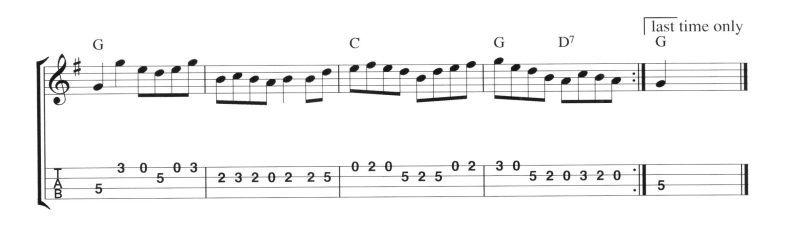

This page has been left blank
to avoid awkward page turns.

The Merry Blacksmith

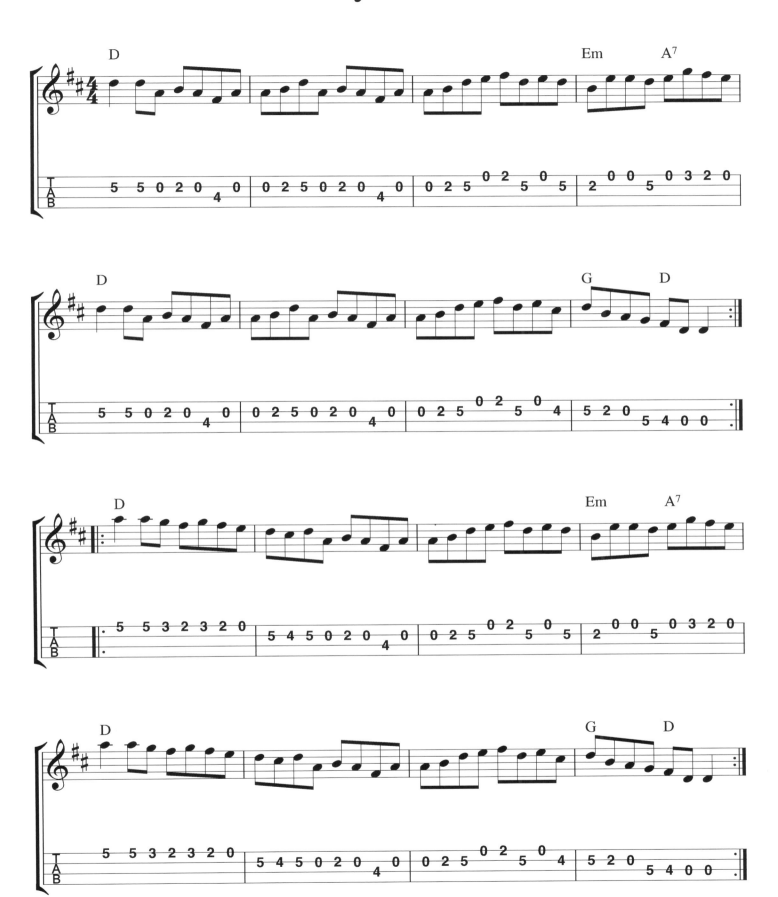

The Star of Munster

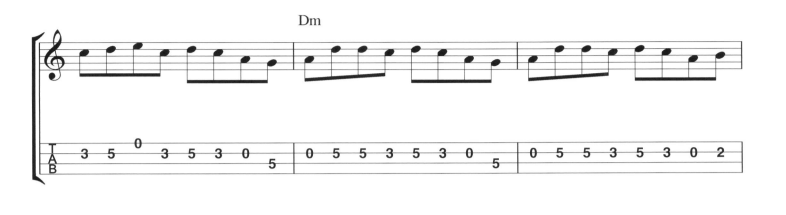